ORGANIZING YOURSELF

Self-coaching questions, inspiration, tips, and practical exercises for becoming an awesome manager

⌘

Managerial Competencies Series
Playbook No. 3

CÉLESTE GRIMARD

Copyright © 2018 Céleste Grimard, Canada

All rights reserved. All materials on these pages are copyrighted by Céleste Grimard. Reproduction, modification, storage of all or part of this book in a retrieval system or retransmission, in any form or by any means, electronic, mechanical, or otherwise is strictly prohibited without prior written permission from the author. Although every effort has been made to indicate the sources of text and ideas, it's possible that we missed some! If you're aware of references or citations that haven't been provided, please contact the author. This book doesn't constitute legal advice and isn't a substitute for independent professional advice.

ISBN-13: 9781979023276

CreateSpace, Charleston, SC USA

⌘
ACKNOWLEDGMENTS

I originally developed this series as a self-study, self-paced program for hundreds of managers working in a geographically dispersed area. Over the span of many years, these awesome managers offered me feedback, inspiration, and encouragement to transform this program into a series of practical, easy to read books accessible to all managers. Thank you! I also sincerely thank Rhiannon Ward for her assistance in editing and proofreading the books in this series.

CONTENTS

Series Introduction   1

Introduction   3

1. Reality Check: Self-Coaching Questions   9

2. Inspiring Your Journey   20

3. Tips for Awesome Managers   30

4. Dilemmas: What Would You Do?   66

5. Planning For Action   74

About the Managerial Competencies Series   76

References   100

ORGANIZING YOURSELF

Welcome to the Managerial Competencies Series!

The aim of this series is to help you understand and build the core competencies you need to become an awesome manager.

There's no getting around it. There are tons of journals, books, blogs, videos – you name it – on the topic of management. Yes, a lot has been written and said about how to be an effective manager. Everyone has their own spin to put on this topic, and research studies on this topic are practically endless. How does a busy

ORGANIZING YOURSELF

manager sort through all the fads and fashions to find the nuggets of wisdom?

In designing this series, I pored over loads of resources and talked with hundreds of managers. I set aside all the fashions, fads, and fantasies, and I extracted only what is likely to be of enduring value to you. Although this series is geared towards practical, immediate use, I hope that it will provoke you to think deeply about managing and your role as a manager, and that it will make a difference for you so you can make a difference for others.

This module – Organizing Yourself – is #3 of 15 books, each covering a key competency of awesome managers. **Turn to page 76 to learn more about this series**, including the full slate of books, how each book is structured, and tips on how to get the most out of them.

Throughout the book, I will refer to your **learning journal** and your **feedback team. These helpful tools are explained on pages 91 and 92.**

ORGANIZING YOURSELF: INTRODUCTION

Awesome managers organize themselves by focusing on their most important priorities and making effective use of their time.

ORGANIZING YOURSELF

Think about a public figure who, in your opinion, seems to have accomplished a great deal in their lifetime; i.e., someone with excellent organizational skills. It could be someone in business, a public figure, a politician, or anyone else you admire. Now think about someone that you know personally who also demonstrates superior organizational skills. In your learning journal, list five specific things that each of these people do regularly or have accomplished that make them role models of organization for you.

Most people are able to spot an organized person. For example, consider Mike, Jordan, Norm, and Sam. Mike and Jordan both supervise staff who spend their days visiting clients. Mike's office is pristinely organized and is remarkable for the general absence of paper. He keeps all paperwork in seven binders on a shelf, and his desk is home only to his computer, his telephone, an in-out basket file, and his planner open to the current day. Mike follows a set routine every day. Most importantly, the first thing and the last thing he does every day is

ORGANIZING YOURSELF

meet with his staff to review the day's assignments. In contrast, Mike's former colleague Jordan had paper covering every square inch of his office: telephone messages, note pads, old lunch bags, and other assorted papers everywhere. He met with his staff sporadically and spent the day dealing with various crises and dramas. When he retired after 25 years of service to his organization, cleaning staff removed 20 bags of recycling and garbage from his office, including miscellaneous papers 10+ years old.

When asked about his organizational strategy, Jordan argued that keeping an office that looked busy made him look hard-working, whereas Mike looked like he didn't have enough work to do. In other words, Jordan believed that looking disorganized protected him from being assigned more work. Although the need to appear busy "for appearance's sake" may seem necessary, generally speaking, an inability to organize one's space and one's time calls into question a person's overall competence.

ORGANIZING YOURSELF

Some organizations require that employees maintain a certain standard of organization. For example, Norm spent half of his time visiting clients and the other half writing reports and doing other paperwork at his desk. His organization provided each staff member with a five-drawer filing cabinet and required that all paperwork (regardless of their degree of confidentiality) be locked in the filing cabinet before they left for lunch breaks and at the end of the day. As a result, Norm became accustomed to maintaining a relatively tidy desk throughout the day so that it would be easy for him to pack it up at the end of the day.

Sam had an entirely different challenge. As a health promotion specialist, he often communicated with people by email. He kept all the e-mails that he received, primarily in his inbox. He also created and stored many documents (including many versions of the same documents) on his computer's desktop. Although his office was fairly neat, his computer was virtually cluttered. Sam forgot to make

ORGANIZING YOURSELF

regular backups of his hard drive or to save documents as he worked on them. Every once in a while, he would experience a crisis: a program would crash, and he would need to rewrite a document from scratch. His failure to delete old versions of documents and unnecessary emails, to use folders to organize his emails and documents, and to perform backups and regular maintenance on his computer caused him to lose valuable time searching for particular e-mails or files or re-creating lost documents.

Since Mike and Norm were able to organize their space and time, their efficiency and effectiveness likely soared above that of Jordan and Sam. The reality of time is that they all have the same amount – just like you and I. At every moment, we are making choices, either consciously or unconsciously, about how to invest that time.

We all probably know people who seem to get a great deal done while others struggle and stress over getting fewer tasks done. One

ORGANIZING YOURSELF

explanation is that there may be systemic issues at play. In other words, some people may have greater access to resources (money, people, technology, etc.) than others, or they may face more constraints on how they use their time. Another explanation is that some people are simply better organized than others. They have a sense of purpose and direction that provides focus to their efforts; they plan their work; they're aware of how they're investing their time; they deal with issues such as email, paperwork and interruptions in an effective manner; they don't procrastinate nor are they perfectionists; and they involve others in getting work done. Although both explanations are legitimate, awesome managers seek to organize themselves despite any barriers they may face.

ORGANIZING YOURSELF

1
REALITY CHECK: SELF COACHING QUESTIONS

To help you examine your organizational skills and challenges, we invite you to ask yourself a series of self-coaching questions. While thinking about your behavior in the past six months, find specific examples that support your answers. Consider whether or not "counter examples"

ORGANIZING YOURSELF

exist; in other words, times when you may not have behaved in a manner that is consistent with your answer. In answering these questions, think about how you generally are rather than temporary aberrations due to stress or other factors.

Your answers to these self-coaching questions will shine a light on how you see yourself. If you know yourself well, your answers will be right on the mark. However, many people don't have accurate self-perceptions because they're not used to assessing themselves, they feel uncomfortable with the idea of reflecting on their own behaviors, or they truly don't know themselves well. As a result, their answers may be *extremely* inflated or low.

In all cases, but especially when answers are extreme (in any direction), seeking candid and honest feedback from others can be a valuable way of shedding light on your actual competency levels. You can learn a lot more about yourself if you get feedback from others.

ORGANIZING YOURSELF

You can ask people to answer some of the self-coaching questions for you and provide examples or anecdotes of situations that illustrate their answers. They may not tell you what you want to hear, but it may be exactly what you need to help you make progress on your journey toward becoming an awesome manager. As American writer Herbert Sebastian Aga said in his book *A Time for Greatness*, "the truth that makes men free is, for the most part, the truth which men prefer not to hear."

Asking others for feedback takes courage on everyone's part. Others don't necessarily have the same picture of you as you have of yourself, and people are sometimes reluctant to "tell it like it is." However, "feedback-lite" that is polite and tells you what you hope to hear won't help you grow as a person. Tell people that you need the straight goods (politely though!).

ORGANIZING YOURSELF

Planning & Priorities

→ Do I have a clearly defined set of life goals in writing?

→ Do I have a similar set of goals for the next six months?

→ Have I done something today to move myself closer to any of my goals?

→ Do I have a clear idea of what I want to accomplish at work during the coming month? Week? Day?

→ Do I try to do the most important tasks during my prime time (when I feel most energetic)?

→ Do I concentrate on objectives, judging myself by accomplishments and results, instead of by amount of activity?

→ Do I set priorities and allocate my time according to importance, not urgency?

→ Do I guard against recurring crises, taking steps to ensure that they don't occur again?

→ Do I set deadlines for myself and my staff?

→ Do I take time to plan?

ORGANIZING YOURSELF

- → Do I make a daily plan?
- → Do I use my time wisely? Or am I guilty of procrastination or perfectionism?
- → Do I anticipate and build in time for interruptions, delays, and so on?
- → Do I tend to realistically evaluate the amount of time a project or task will take?

People

- → Do I set and follow an agenda in meetings? And do I maintain control of the meeting?
- → Do I delegate as much work as possible?
- → Do I delegate challenging tasks, as well as routine ones?
- → Do I delegate authority along with responsibility?
- → Do I prevent staff from delegating upward those decisions and tasks that they find difficult or worrisome?
- → Do I make effective use of my staff to gain better control of my time?

ORGANIZING YOURSELF

Patterns & Practices

→ Do I try to handle matters by phone or in person whenever I have a choice, using written communication only when it's essential for record keeping purposes?

→ Do I avoid thinking about work when I'm not at work?

→ Do I make minor decisions quickly?

→ In the past six months, have I evaluated my time usage and discontinued unproductive routines or activities?

→ Do I keep things in my bag or briefcase that I can work on whenever I get spare moments: line-ups, waiting rooms, planes?

→ Do I try to live in the present, thinking in terms of what needs to be done now instead of rehashing past errors or successes or worrying about the future?

→ Am I continually striving to establish habits that will make me more effective?

→ Do I apply Pareto's 80/20 Principle whenever I'm confronted with several different tasks

ORGANIZING YOURSELF

that need to be done? Do I focus my efforts on the critical activities where I can have a big impact? (Pareto, a 19th century Italian economist, noted that, in almost any human endeavor, 80% of results come about through 20% of efforts, and, conversely, approximately 80% of the efforts produce 20% of the results.)

→ Am I really in control of my time? Are my actions determined primarily by me, not by circumstances or other people's priorities?

→ Do I keep my eye on the big picture? Or do I get bogged down in details?

→ Can I recognize my own limits? Or do I attempt to take on too much? Can I say *no*?

→ Do I know where things are when I need them? Or do I spend time searching for files or information?

→ Can I keep myself focused? Or do I get distracted and interrupt myself often?

→ Do I have good self-control? Or does emotional upset sometimes slow me down?

ORGANIZING YOURSELF

- → Do I perform effectively? Or do I let perfectionism or laziness hold me back?
- → Do I keep things professional at work? Or do I sometimes socialize too much when I should be on task?
- → Do I have a system in place for dealing with paperwork and emails? Or do I handle them twice or even more often?
- → Do I avoid these habits of ineffective people identified by John Covey (in Stephen Covey's book on effective people):
  - → Be reactive. Fight fires. Avoid planning.
  - → Work without a clear goal in mind.
  - → Do urgent things first.
  - → Fear change and put off improvement.

ORGANIZING YOURSELF

Workplace Organization

→ Is my office layout optimized for the right balance of collaboration and productivity?

→ Is my workplace structure clear and stable? Or are people confused about their roles, responsibilities, and authority levels?

→ Are communication guidelines in place? Or am I and staff often delayed by unnecessary interruptions or confusion?

→ Does my workplace have stable priorities or guiding principles? Or do shifting priorities slow things down?

→ Are meetings purposeful and structured?

→ Can staff handle the workload?

→ Are files, office supplies, work stations, etc. optimally organized?

→ Do I have an orientation and training system in place for new staff?

→ Do staff have the equipment, supplies, and other resources needed to do their work?

→ Are expectations clear, and do I offer plenty of support to staff?

ORGANIZING YOURSELF

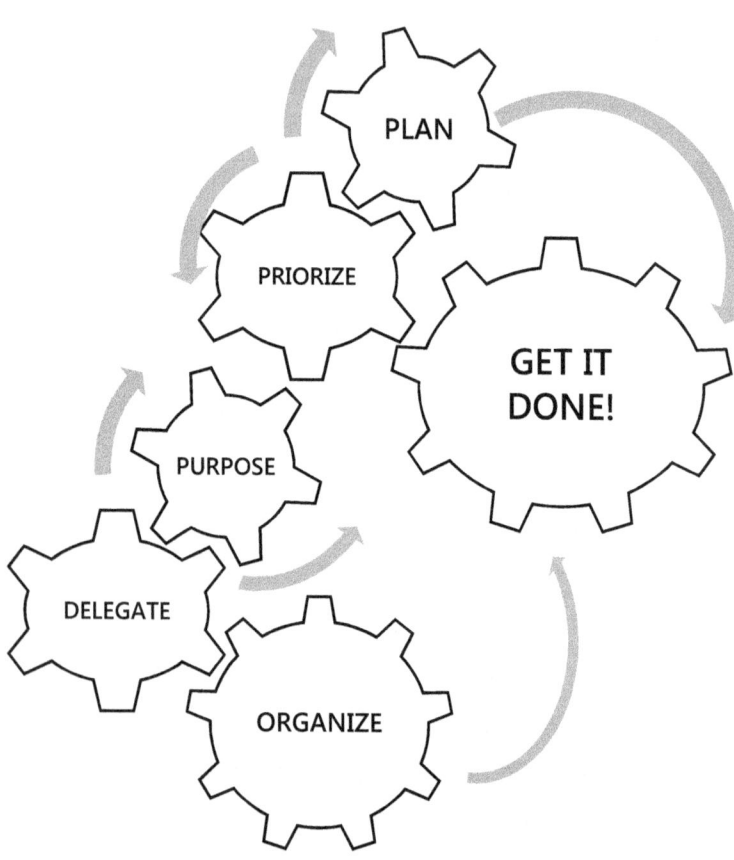

ORGANIZING YOURSELF

Reflection

What do your answers say about your perceptions of your organizing strengths and opportunities for improvement? Do you consider yourself to be a well-organized person? Do you invest your time well? Are you thoughtful about your working habits? Or do you feel like you're messy, haphazard, and prone to distraction? What feedback have others given you about your level of organization? How much overlap is there between your personal view and others' opinions? If they don't overlap well, why might this be the case? What about your workplace? Does it function smoothly? Or have you thought of ways that it could work better for everyone?

    Whether you feel like a well-oiled machine at work, or if you think you need to clean up your desk, office environment, or work habits, the important thing is to use this reflection as an opportunity to make improvements…now!

ORGANIZING YOURSELF

2

INSPIRING YOUR JOURNEY

As you read through the following quotations, take note of the ones that speak to you the most. Then consider the message they are conveying to you.

ORGANIZING YOURSELF

We have time enough if we will but use it alright.
Johann Wolfgang von Goethe

⌘

Doing more things is no substitute for doing the right things.
Anonymous

⌘

I try to take one day at a time, but sometimes several days attack me at once. I could do great things, if I weren't so busy doing little things.
Ashleigh Brilliant

⌘

An hour in the morning is worth two in the evening.
Proverbs

⌘

A person without a goal is like a ship without a rudder.
Anonymous

ORGANIZING YOURSELF

It is through our habits that we are choosing much more than what we will do in this moment; rather, we are choosing the direction we are setting for ourselves.
Russell Connors & Patrick McCormick

⌘

I recommend you to take care of the minutes: for hours will take care of themselves.
Earl of Chesterfield

⌘

Our life is frittered away by detail. Simplify.
Henry David Thoreau

⌘

The world is too much with us; late and soon, getting and spending, we lay waste our powers.
William Woodsworth

⌘

If opportunity doesn't knock, build a door.
Milton Berle

ORGANIZING YOURSELF

Don't wait for your ship to come in; swim out to it.
Unknown

⌘

Anything worth doing is worth doing now.
Ralph Stayer

⌘

Besides the noble art of getting things done, there is the noble art of leaving things undone. The wisdom of life consists in the elimination of non-essentials.
Chinese proverb

⌘

The reason most major goals are not achieved is that we spend our time doing second things first.
Robert McCain

⌘

Nothing is so fatiguing as the eternal hanging on of an uncompleted task.
William James

ORGANIZING YOURSELF

You can see that basically our lives are, to a large extent, spent in avoiding confrontation with ourselves. And then you can begin to make sense of the enormous amount of culture's daily activities, which attempt to distract us from ourselves, from a deep reflection, from deep thinking, from existential confrontation. There's a wonderful phrase by the philosopher Kierkegaard, 'tranquillization by the trivial.'
Roy Walsh

⌘

The wisdom of life consists in the elimination of non-essentials.
Lin Yutang

⌘

We can't be happy if we expect to live all the time at the highest peak of intensity. Happiness isn't a question of intensity, but of equilibrium, order, rhythm, and harmony.
Thomas Merton

ORGANIZING YOURSELF

When your work environment is messy, there is often chaos in your mind. Tidy up your immediate work environment, and you will see order show up in your life!
Paul Rousseau

⌘

A person who does not think and plan long ahead will find trouble right by his door.
Confucius

⌘

Delay is the deadliest form of denial.
C. Northcote Parkinson

⌘

Most of us say yes to too much stuff, and then we let these little, mediocre things fill our lives.
Derek Sivers

⌘

The best way to predict the future is to create it.
Peter Drucker

ORGANIZING YOURSELF

The wisdom of life consists in the elimination of non-essentials.
Lin Yutang

⌘

No one ever got rich checking their email more often.
Noah Kagan

⌘

Turn off your email; turn off your phone; disconnect from the Internet. Figure out a way to set limits so you can concentrate when you need to and disengage when you need to. Technology is a good servant but a bad master.
Gretchen Rubin

⌘

Could you spend a week or even a day without reading your emails, using social media or going online? Someone recently joked with me that having Internet access is more important than having food or water.
Nigel Cumberland

ORGANIZING YOURSELF

Man who stand on hill with mouth open will wait long time for roast duck to drop in.
Confucius

⌘

The best way to get something done is to begin.
Anonymous

⌘

The difference between great people and everyone else is that great people create their lives actively, while everyone else is created by their lives, passively waiting to see where life takes them next. The difference between the two is the difference between living fully and just existing.
Michael Gerber, Think & Grow Rich

ORGANIZING YOURSELF

Consider the following quotation from *The Stress Examiner:*

If you had a bank that credited your account each morning with $86,000 that carried over no balance from day to day, allowed you to keep no cash in your accounts, and every evening cancelled whatever part of the amount you had failed to use during the day, what would you do? Draw out every cent every day, of course, and use it to your advantage! You do have such a bank: Time! Every morning, it credits you with 86,400 seconds. Every night, it writes off as lost whatever of this you have failed to invest to good purpose. It carries over no balances. It allows no overdrafts. Each day, it opens a new account with you. Each night, it burns the records of the day. There is no going back. There is no drawing against tomorrow's time. It is up to each of us to invest this precious fund of hours, minutes, and seconds in order to get from it the utmost in health, happiness and success!

ORGANIZING YOURSELF

What are your five favorite quotations?

Why do these stand out for you?

Which would you want to adopt as your personal motto? Include on the signature line of your emails? Post on your desk?

ORGANIZING YOURSELF

3

TIPS FOR AWESOME MANAGERS

As you review the following tips for organizing your time and yourself, circle, check or highlight those that are especially meaningful for you.

ORGANIZING YOURSELF

1. **Keep in mind that you and the super productive person and the terribly unproductive person next to you all have the same amount of time at your disposal every day.** There is nothing that we can do to literally manage time. The clock ticks away at 60 seconds a minute. There are 60 minutes an hour no matter what we do. The key is how you choose to use your time. Our own behavior is the only thing that we really have control over, and having the discipline to control our behavior is the key to effective time management.

2. **Focus on being effective.** "Efficiency" means doing things right (without waste), and "effectiveness" means doing the right things right. Evaluate your work in terms of your results (not activity levels). Being busy doesn't necessarily mean that we're accomplishing what we should be accomplishing. The challenge is to be effective.

ORGANIZING YOURSELF

3. **Invest your time as though it was a precious resource**, because that's what it is! Without time, you don't have any other resources.

4. **Avoid putting in more time in tasks than you should just because you "have the time" to do so.** Remember (and avoid) Parkinson's first law: People expand work to fill the time available. Most tasks aren't completed until just prior to deadlines. If we know that a task doesn't have to be finished for one week, it will usually take us that week to finish it. Set reasonable deadlines and goals, and work towards accomplishing those goals.

5. **Invest your time in accomplishing your big priorities.** Avoid falling pretty to Parkinson's second law: Time is usually expended in amounts inversely proportional to the importance of the tasks.

ORGANIZING YOURSELF

6. **Own up to where you're really spending your time.** People often think that they spend their time on their priorities, but that's not usually the case. They are seldom aware of how they are truly using their time.

7. **Find out where your time is *really* going so that you can take more control of your use of time.** Keep a log of your time use in 15 minute blocks during two typical work days.
   a. Start each day by listing your top five priorities for the day along with your estimate of how much time it will take to accomplish each one. Here's an example:

Priorities for the day	Estimated time to accomplish
1. Finish Report X	3 hours
2. Respond to client request	½ hour
Etc.	

ORGANIZING YOURSELF

b. Then, create a log to record the time, your actual activities and the importance of each (for example: A = Vital, B = Important, C = Limited Value, D = Wasted Time). Here's an example:

Time	Activity	Priority
8:00	Checking & organizing email inbox	B
8:15	Research and calculations for Report X	A
9:00	Chatted with colleague Z over coffee	D
Etc.		

c. Now, classify each of your activities on your completed time logs as follows:
1. Something that you MUST do
2. Something that you SHOULD do but with someone else's help
3. Something that you COULD do but that others could learn to do

ORGANIZING YOURSELF

4. Something that OTHERS SHOULD do
5. Something that OTHERS MUST do
6. Something that you did that wasn't necessary for accomplishing your priorities.

d. Next, summarize your average use of time over the two days by using a 24-hour pie diagram. Divide the pie into slices of appropriate size given the amount of time you spent on each type of work activity. Include slices of time for meals and coffee breaks, personal hygiene, sleep, travel to and from work, and any other activities from your day.

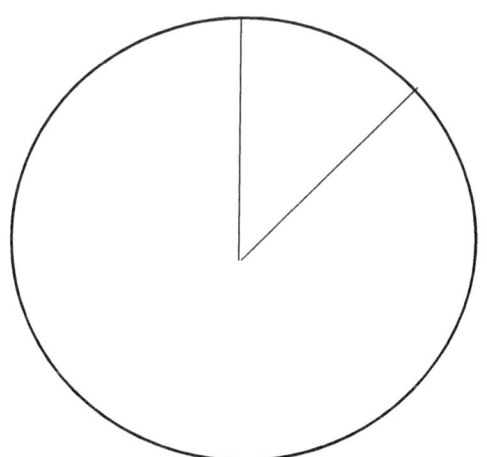

ORGANIZING YOURSELF

e. To identify how to gain better control of your time, eliminate time wasters, and delegate (where possible), review your time logs, and ask yourself:
   i. How many of your activities are in categories 2, 3, 4, and 5? These all represent opportunities for delegation.
   ii. Did identifying your priorities for each day help you accomplish them? Why or why not? Was your estimate of the amount of time required to accomplish them accurate? If not, why?
   iii. Look at all the demands on your time. When did they occur? What did they involve? Which demands are likely to increase? Decrease? Which required no immediate action? What are your persistent time wasters? What did you do that really helped you manage your time?
   iv. Where do you seem to be spending most of your time? What patterns can you identify?

ORGANIZING YOURSELF

8. **Plan your work, then work your plan!** Many of us spend a great deal of time carrying out activities for which we have done very little planning. Daily planning – whether first thing in the morning or last thing of the day - is essential. Every hour spent in effective planning saves three to four in execution and achieves better results.

9. **Use your calendar/planner to record your commitments.** Calendars reinforce the habit of doing one thing at a time. If you don't jot down an upcoming appointment, you'll keep reminding yourself about it, and it will occupy "room" in your brain that could be used for something else. If you promise to phone someone in three weeks, note the commitment in your calendar immediately.

10. **Plan for relaxation and renewal.** To prevent burnout, people need to "plan not to plan."

ORGANIZING YOURSELF

11. **Use the 100th birthday technique to develop long-term objectives.** Imagine that a reporter is interviewing you on your 100th birthday. The reporter asks you to name the things that you're most proud of and where you directed your efforts in life.
    a. Visualize the end result as if it had already happened, and answer this question as specifically as possible. Here are some possible categories: career, family, community, spirituality, health, learning, financial assets, leisure and travel, and personal relationships.
    b. Identify intermediate goals based on your 100th birthday goals: 10 years from now, five years from now, and one year from now.
    c. Identify specific short-term goals for the next six months. Develop action steps and deadlines for undertaking them.
    d. Review and revise your goals regularly.

ORGANIZING YOURSELF

12. **Make realistic time estimates, and build in extra time for unforeseen snags.** In setting deadlines, expect the unexpected, and allow time for handling emergencies, seizing opportunities, and dealing with your own and others' errors. Remember Murphy's Laws:
    a. Everything takes 20% longer than you think it will take.
    b. Nothing is as simple as it seems.
    c. If anything can go wrong, it will.

13. **Don't fall into the habit of simply doing what's familiar and routine.** Remember Gresham's law: Other factors being equal, the desire to avoid anxiety will cause an individual to repeat familiar patterns and shun innovative activities.

14. **Identify your priorities!** Your priorities need to be clear in order to make reasonable decisions about where to invest your time.

Allocate time to tasks in proportion to the priority of anticipated results.

15. **Distinguish between important and urgent tasks.** Stephen Covey's priority matrix is a helpful tool for identifying those activities that demand immediate attention (urgent), those that contribute to high-priority goals (important), those that are both, and those that are neither (see the table on the next page). Focusing on quadrant 2 is an effective way of shrinking the size of quadrants 3 and 4 and avoid falling into the crises of quadrant 1.

ORGANIZING YOURSELF

1 Urgent and important	2 Important but not urgent
Crises Pressing problems Deadline-driven projects	Relationship building Recognizing new opportunities Planning
3 Urgent but not important	4 Neither urgent nor important
Interruptions Some calls Some mail, reports	Trivia, busy work Some mail/calls Time wasters

16. **Keep your priorities in mind...relentlessly!** People tend to respond to immediate pressures or the present moment's demands. As a result, they lose sight of the consequences of neglecting important tasks.

ORGANIZING YOURSELF

17. **Prepare a daily to-do list.** Prioritize the items on your to-do list, and make tasks meet both the importance and urgency tests. Important tasks seldom need doing right now, while urgent tasks disguise minor requirements as major ones or "crises." Ask yourself, "What two or three critical tasks must I get done today to feel like I've had a super productive day?" Put these tasks at the top of your list, and schedule time for them. Also, note which to-do items stay on your list day after day. Delegate these or break them down into smaller units for handling efficiently.

18. **Don't put second things first.** Learn to distinguish between what must be done, what could be done, and what you would like to do. Follow Pareto's Principle – devote more time to the vital few situations or problems and accomplish more.

ORGANIZING YOURSELF

19. **Stop firefighting.** Be honest with yourself. Do you thrive on firefighting and hence encourage "arsonists?" Analyze which situations warrant an investment in fire prevention. Include the firefighting process in your time planning. Delegate whenever possible.

20. **Eliminate trivia, even if you like doing it.** Ask yourself: "Would I pay my assistant good money to do the same task?" "What is the best use of my time right now?" "Would anything terrible happen if I didn't do this?"

21. **Use your time for happiness.** A million dollar idea can't buy your child's smile or stop a heart attack.

22. **Evaluate your work in terms of your results.** Sometimes, people evaluate work in terms of activity instead of results. But, remember, being busy isn't the same as being productive.

ORGANIZING YOURSELF

23. **Group similar tasks together in manageable chunks** as a way of minimizing interruptions and benefiting from the efficiency of repetitive action. Also, sub-divide large tasks into smaller tasks to increase the satisfaction that comes with finishing a task.

24. **Reserve blocks of time in your day to work on your priorities.** Activities are generally completed most effectively when they're not interrupted. Give yourself regular periods of uninterrupted concentration so that you can plan and carry out top priority tasks. One undistracted hour is worth two to four typical hours. Don't try to get the most important jobs done in short time bursts sandwiched between trivia. Let the trivial items fill in around your blocked times. Many people only put appointments or deadlines in their calendars, but it's important to designate blocks of time for your priorities.

ORGANIZING YOURSELF

25. **Schedule your work according to your prime time: your body's internal clock that governs your daily energy and personal efficiency levels.** Focus on your top priority work when you're at your peak energy level.

26. **Avoid the trap of reverse delegation.** This form of upward delegation happens when employees seek answers from their managers that they should already have. These employees may be afraid of criticism or taking risks, or they may lack confidence or the information and resources needed to do their work. Managers who "need to be needed" encourage this type of behavior by always saying *yes* to requests for help rather than teaching employees to do their own problem solving and solution finding.

27. **Delegate properly.**
    → Managers who can't delegate effectively can't manage effectively. Delegation extends results beyond what an

ORGANIZING YOURSELF

individual can do to what the individual can control. It develops staff initiative, skill, knowledge, and competence.

→ Identify how much time you spend managing versus doing what others could do. Don't succumb to the myth of the perfectionist (if you want something done right, you have to do it yourself). If you do a task yourself, you're only ensuring that you will have to do it yourself the next time. As long as you keep certain tasks to yourself, you don't teach someone else to do them, and that usually only increases your frustration and responsibilities.

→ Managers who spend time doing things their staff should be doing, give incomplete instructions, keep staff waiting, needlessly interrupt their work, or communicate poorly create time management problems for their staff.

→ Delegate decisions and responsibilities to the lowest comfortable level possible.

ORGANIZING YOURSELF

→ Delegate responsibility and (crystal clear) authority for whole tasks, especially when staff are motivated, skilled and experienced. Be sure to offer performance feedback on a regular basis so that objectives are maintained, and staff feel that you recognize their efforts.

28. **Help your staff manage their time.** Don't simply assume that they know how to do so. Also, if you have corrected your own bad habits and learned to manage your time, you will set an excellent example for staff.

29. **Remember that indecision is a decision not to decide.** Procrastination and indecision usually result from an unrealistic need to know all the facts. But if all the facts were known, a decision wouldn't have to be made; the course of action would be self-evident. Many people spend more time putting things off due to under-confidence and indecision than they actually spend in

ORGANIZING YOURSELF

doing the tasks themselves. Procrastination can cause lost opportunity, increased pressure, and damaged relationships. You will gain more respect (including self-respect), if you impose deadlines on yourself and have the courage to take a stand, especially for challenging decisions. By the way, postponing an important decision (such as taking on a project) is the same as saying *no*.

30. **Take responsibility for your own decisions,** including decisions about the allocation of your time. Keep in mind that more effective results are achieved by systematically applying effort toward a planned objective than by chance. Also, keep your goals and objectives visible (for example, on a sheet of paper posted on the wall). This will increase the likelihood of reaching them.

ORGANIZING YOURSELF

31. **Try to anticipate potential problems by reflecting on past experience.** Deal with small problems before they explode into full blown emergencies. Remember: A stitch in time saves nine!

32. **Get started on a task, and stick with it**. It's a matter of discipline. Have you ever started some work first thing in the morning, been interrupted by a phone call asking for information you don't have but one of your employees does have, dropped the work you were doing to get the information, and been distracted by a conversation on the way, which led to the coffee machine? By 10:00 a.m., you suddenly realize that the only thing you finished so far today was your cup of coffee!

33. **Look at challenging tasks in a different way**: "If I don't act, it will become a crisis." Problems always introduce fear, but a crisis is an even bigger problem. When mental

ORGANIZING YOURSELF

blocks occur, talk it out with someone you trust. Ask yourself, "What am I avoiding?" Then, try to address the problem directly.

34. **Give yourself frequent, small rewards** for accomplishing difficult tasks. Even small breaks can serve as rewards.

35. **Use the salami technique**: Salami, in its original state, is too big to bite into. But cut it into thin slices, and it looks manageable. So, if you're having trouble getting started on a big project, slice it into small, manageable "instant tasks" or small steps. Ask yourself, "What's the first step of this project (collecting material, thinking about how to approach the task)?" After taking the first step, other steps become clearer and easier. This will help you build momentum.

36. **Refer to unpleasant tasks that must be done as "garbage."** We don't like looking at garbage and keeping it around. If you

ORGANIZING YOURSELF

reframe undesirable tasks as garbage, you may be more willing to "take it out" sooner.

37. **Use the "do nothing" technique.** When something must absolutely be done, but you can't bring yourself to work on it, do nothing for 10 minutes. But first, place the half-completed project or whatever it is you're trying to avoid right in front of you, and stare at it. You'll hate the task, and you'll want to push it aside. Then, you'll finally decide to get rid of it by doing it.

38. **To discourage procrastination, use the balance sheet method.** On the left side of a sheet of paper, list all the reasons you're procrastinating on a particular task. On the right side, list all the benefits that will accrue if you get the job done. Typically, on the left side, there's only one or two excuses, such as "I might be bored," or "It might involve an awkward confrontation." On the other side, there's often a long list of benefits, including

the feeling of relief that comes with getting a necessary but unpleasant task done and out of the way.

39. **Keep your desk top clean.** Organize your desk so that paper shuffling is minimized, and the material that you need to access is within reach. Beware of the "stacked desk syndrome." Usually, stacked items become a constant source of mental interruption and anxiety. Arrange your projects on a priority basis. Have a file for things to do as soon as possible, another for semi-urgent items, another for "would like to" items, and possibly another for informational reading. Designate files in any way that suits your needs and priorities, but keep these files off your desk. Keep on your desk only the project you're working on. Don't allow other files on your desk until you're ready to work on them. Use the same ideas for organizing your computer's desktop.

ORGANIZING YOURSELF

40. **Set aside a block of time to "houseclean" accumulated paper, files, and office supplies.** Use the wastebasket, shredder, and recycle bin with courage. Don't waste time reading or filing irrelevant material.

41. **Handle your in-basket items at a fixed time each day**. Sort as you open your mail with the wastebasket/recycle bin close at hand. Handle each letter only once. Don't simply shuffle paper around. Do whatever has to be done. Single handling requires practice and a strong will to avoid getting sidetracked by items where information is incomplete. Refer these items to the proper place to get the needed information.

42. **Work on one thing at a time.** Follow-through is simply a continuation of single handling – the habit of doing one thing at a time and staying with it until it's finished. Don't abandon your project for something more interesting or attractive until it's completed

and disposed of. When it's on its way, check your priorities and start the next project.

43. **Manage your emails, before they manage you!**
    → Start your day with your own priorities, and block off specific times to check your email; for example, once every two hours. Outside of these blocks of time, resist the urge to check your email.
    → If you can reply to an email within five minutes, do it! Otherwise, schedule a time to respond to it in your planner.
    → Don't send an email when you're angry. Sleep on it overnight if possible.
    → Unsubscribe from mailing lists.

44. **Improve your reading skills.** Managers often need to do extensive reading in handling their daily affairs and keeping current in their technical fields. Learn how to scan material rapidly in order to determine what needs reading more carefully.

ORGANIZING YOURSELF

45. **Keep a notebook handy** to record random notes, and jot down ideas, reminders from old papers, old notes to yourself and old to-do lists. Integrate and prioritize these with your current priority and to do lists.

46. **Ask those around you for their tips on getting organized and managing time.** You never know what you might learn!

47. **Learn to say *no* to requests.** Remember that it's impossible to achieve excellence without concentrating your effort on critical areas. Every project is on someone's "must" list, but that doesn't make it your priority. If it must be done, let someone else do it.

48. **Control socializing.** Prolonged discussion of personal affairs, sports events, last night's TV show, etc., are monumental time wasters.

49. **Analyze your incoming phone calls.** Prepare and complete a call interruption analysis

ORGANIZING YOURSELF

form. If you're frequently receiving calls that you have to refer to other people or that are simply unnecessary, determine what you can do to cut down on them.

50. **Manage your phone usage:**
    a. Keep a contact list handy, physically or digitally.
    b. Use an agenda before making calls: name, topic, purpose, goals.
    c. Don't accept calls during times you set aside for "solitary" work (except in emergencies).
    d. "Bunch" your phone calls; ask what the best or worst time to call would be.
    e. Set the tone of the conversation at the beginning: "What can I do for you?" rather than: "How are things going?"
    f. Have someone screen calls if possible.
    g. Use conference calls whenever you have to repeat the same message to three or more people.

ORGANIZING YOURSELF

    h. Don't spend too much time on hold; hang up if you've been put on hold for an excessive amount of time.

    i. For long-winded people:
        i. Be honest; say, "I don't have the time to talk now."
        ii. Set a kitchen timer/buzzer.
        iii. Indicate that someone's on the other line.
        iv. Don't hesitate to interrupt them, and end the call if your attempts to keep things brief fail.

51. **Analyze why and when "drop-ins" occur, and manage them.**
    → Jot down notes on conversations held and their *yield*. This may help you curtail your time with certain people and increase it with others.
    → Avoid instant discussions even in supposed emergencies.
    → Reserve hours for visitors, if possible.

ORGANIZING YOURSELF

→ Keep in mind that, when concentrating on a task and upon being interrupted, the average person needs approximately 18 minutes to return to their level of concentration prior to the interruption.

→ Close the door, when needed. Be aware that a continuously open door invites disruption. It's possible to be accessible to others and still have certain times when your door is closed. The critical issue is not the door itself but how you handle the situation.

→ Use door flags. Place a colored flag on the door – red, yellow, green – to show people how available you are for visitors.

→ Suggest that you meet in a conference room or another person's office. When staff want to see you, offer to go to their work area instead. This allows you to control the time better, and the materials you might require will be close at hand. Schedule regular meetings with staff as a

ORGANIZING YOURSELF

way of minimizing impromptu visits from them.

→ Meet visitors outside your office.
→ Confer by standing up. Try to greet unexpected visitors outside your office or by standing. Alternatively, stand up to signal the end of a conversation.
→ Have someone screen visitors.
→ Set the agenda early in a conversation.
→ Help "time wasters" out of your office. Almost all time wasters announce that they're leaving long before they actually do it. Simply reply, "Before you leave, there's something I must show you." It can be anything – an announcement on a bulletin board, the company art collection, etc. – but it must be out of the office. Then simply say good-bye and move decisively toward your door. Don't let the conversation start up again.
→ Be honest with drop-ins including your boss. Explain that you're trying to get better control of your time, and ask if you

could arrange mutually convenient times each day to check with each other on routine matters.
- → Develop a system for dealing with interruptions.
- → Learn to do these things naturally, without coming across as rude!

52. **If your job allows it, consider spending an occasional morning or even a full day working at home** where interruptions are less likely.

53. **If you call a meeting, manage it effectively:**
    a. Avoid the "let's call a meeting" habit. Start eliminating one meeting each month, then one per week. See if work still progresses.
    b. Meet for information, training, control, motivation, or decision-making. If a proposed meeting doesn't fall into one of these categories, question it.

ORGANIZING YOURSELF

c. Distribute an agenda before the meeting. List the people who will participate, the problems to discuss, and the information or solutions each person should bring. Check that participants are prepared prior to the meeting.
d. Ensure that the meeting's purpose and agenda are posted for all to see (whiteboard, PowerPoint, etc.).
e. Don't permit interruptions such as calls or notifications.
f. Ask an assistant to take notes and arrange for follow-up.
g. Set a time limit, preferably 20-60 minutes maximum.
h. Hold meetings late in the day, before lunch, or Friday afternoon.
i. Make all participants stick to the agenda.
j. Get closure on each item.
k. At the end of meeting, summarize decisions reached and assignments made.

ORGANIZING YOURSELF

l. Record meeting minutes and distribute to participants and interested people. Include all decisions, responsibilities, action steps, and deadlines established during meeting.

m. Follow-up on action items.

54. **Start and end meetings on time.** Don't wait for the chronic latecomer. Assume that when people are late, they won't be showing up at all. Tell them this is what you'll conclude. Having warned them in advance, be firm about it. They'll soon get the message.

55. **Manage your participation in meetings that others call.** If the meeting isn't following tips 53 and 54:

    a. Suggest an agenda for the next meeting.
    b. Suggest a completion or ending time privately.
    c. Keep minutes of the meeting if no one else is.

ORGANIZING YOURSELF

   d. Help pull together ideas by asking "What have we decided about…?"
   e. Help keep the meeting on track by speaking up.
   f. Be prepared for the meeting.

56. **Don't overlook blocks of time that pop up during the day.** No period is so short that you can't use it productively. It takes only five minutes to make an appointment, send an email, or write a note. It takes only 10 minutes to make one or two brief phone calls, organize a small pile of papers on your desk, or read a brief report. It takes fewer than 30 minutes to outline a report, skim journals or newspapers, or organize a stack of papers. Also, use waiting time constructively (to read, relax, or plan something).

ORGANIZING YOURSELF

57. **Practice Alan Lakein's unique time savers.** Here's a sampling of them:
    a. I try to enjoy whatever I'm doing.
    b. I don't waste time regretting my failures.
    c. I remind myself: "There's always enough time for the important things." If it's important, I'll make the time to do it.
    d. I don't own a television set.
    e. I work alone creatively in the morning and use the afternoons for meetings, if necessary.
    f. I try not to waste other people's time (unless it's something that really matters to me).
    g. I have a place for everything (so I waste as little time as possible looking for things).
    h. I save up all trivia for a three-hour session once a month.
    i. I don't think of work on weekends.
    j. I relax and "do nothing" frequently.

ORGANIZING YOURSELF

After reading these tips, review the ones that you have circled, checked, or highlighted. What do they have in common?

4

DILEMMAS: WHAT WOULD YOU DO?

This section gives you the opportunity to consider how to apply what you've just learned to two situations. Read and complete each exercise. Then, in your learning journal, explain why you answered the way you did and how you might apply this at work.

ORGANIZING YOURSELF

Exercise 1: Setting Priorities

(This exercise was adapted from the book, *Right on Time*.)

Imagine that it's a typical day for you. You arrive at work and find that there are 12 items in your *inbox* (arriving via mail, fax, email, and/or voice mail) that require your attention. Your challenge is deciding what to do with each item using the following priority codes:

A1   Do first!
A   Top priority items
B   Medium priority items
C   Low priority items
13   Wastebasket

For each item, assign what you consider to be an appropriate priority code. You can use the same code multiple times and even assign two priority codes for an item (if there are two actions that you will take in relation to that item).

ORGANIZING YOURSELF

1. ____ Your manager left a voice mail indicating that she would like a reply within the next few minutes.

2. ____ You receive a generic fax offering seat sales on trips to Vegas. You don't have any plans to go there soon.

3. ____ A safety officer sends you a form via interoffice mail that you need to sign and return by next week.

4. ____ You receive an invitation to a retirement party for an employee in another work unit. They want an R.S.V.P. by the end of the day.

5. ____ The chair of the Quality Assurance Committee emails you a copy of the agenda for a meeting that you already knew about that is scheduled for two weeks from today.

ORGANIZING YOURSELF

6. ____ Your colleague in another city sends you a note indicating that there will be a four-way conference call in which you need to participate next Wednesday at 10:30 a.m.

7. ____ A coworker sends you an article that he clipped from a magazine along with the note, "This is good stuff. Enjoy!"

8. ____ The chair of the Community Relations Committee, of which you're a member, wants you to provide some numbers from your operation by this afternoon so that she can get going on a report that is due in three weeks.

9. ____ You have a payroll form to complete within the next two weeks.

ORGANIZING YOURSELF

10. ____ You notice that the latest issue of a trade magazine has arrived. You especially enjoy reading this magazine because it helps you stay up-to-date with developments in your field.

11. ____ You receive an emailed advertisement for a piece of equipment that you're unlikely to use in your work unit.

12. ____ You receive a report from the accounting office detailing your work unit's expenditures in the past month. You need to review the report and notify the accounting office of any inaccuracies by the end of the month.

Now, review your choices. How much confidence do you have in your choices? Do you have items in every category? What was the most challenging part of assigning priority codes? How might you apply this type of analysis to your work?

ORGANIZING YOURSELF

Exercise 2: Organizing Your Day

(This exercise was adapted from *Twenty Active Training Programs Volume II*.)

Suppose that you're the manager of a medical laboratory. As you begin an average day, you estimate the total amount of time each task on your to-do list will take if you do everything yourself. Here's your un-prioritized list:

1. Have lunch with your boss, the CEO: **1 hour**

2. Prepare a budget for the following year; get preliminary information first: **2-3 days**

3. Organize inbox: **1-1.5 hours**

4. Prepare for managers' meeting with the CEO at 3:00 p.m.: **1 hour**

5. Answer urgent correspondence: **1 hour**

6. Return 10 phone calls to doctors: **1-1.5 hours**

ORGANIZING YOURSELF

7. Get more information on new lab testing instruments being piloted by a supplier. Investigate the possibility that they're similar to instruments you recently proposed to the CEO: **1 hour**

8. Check out a rumor that something's wrong with your computer printout of the results of lab test X: **unsure**

9. Review proposal from respected technician for new policies and procedures: **1 hour**

10. Double-check statistics from latest study for possible need to revise the procedure for conducting a certain lab test: **2-3 days**

11. Obtain needed reference material, and prepare a presentation for an upcoming conference: **2 hours**

12. Read the trade journals piling up on your desk: **unsure**

ORGANIZING YOURSELF

Your task is to plan your day using Stephen Covey's priority matrix approach (see tip 15). First determine which items belong in each quadrant. Then, decide when you will address them during the course of your day. Each of the 12 items must be at least partially addressed or completed within a regular work day. You have an assistant and two associates who work for you.

Now, reflect on your experience. What was the most challenging part of the exercise? How many tasks did you delegate to your staff? If you delegated items, did you remember to schedule the time needed to explain them and follow up? How might you apply this type of analysis to your work?

5

PLANNING FOR ACTION

In your learning journal:
1. Describe the top three challenges you personally face in organizing yourself and managing your time. What are they? What are the root causes of these challenges? How are they impacting your productivity and effectiveness?

ORGANIZING YOURSELF

2. What tips and ideas from this book can you apply to help you address those challenges?
3. Starting now, what five specific actions will you take to address these challenges and improve your overall level of organization and time management?
4. Starting now, what five specific actions will you take to help your staff get organized and manage their time effectively?

ORGANIZING YOURSELF

About the Managerial Competencies Series

What's in the series?

This series is built around four managerial competency clusters: personal, people, purpose, and process.

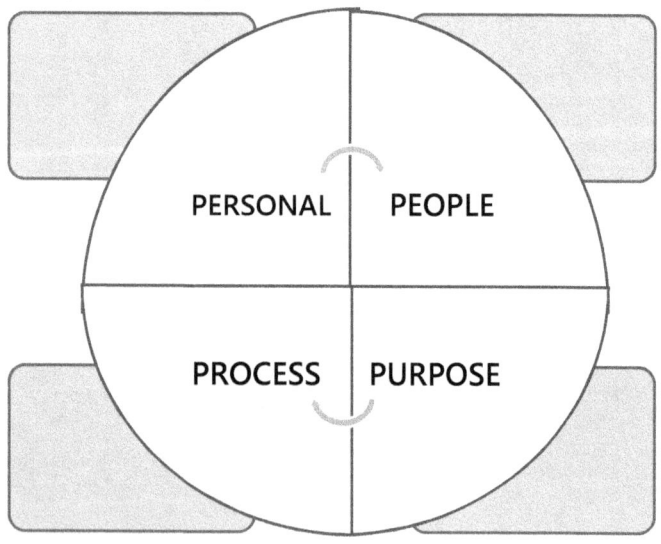

ORGANIZING YOURSELF

Each cluster is made up of several competencies possessed by awesome managers. The series addresses a total of 15 competencies, each of which is the topic of a book of around 100 pages. Let's look at each cluster one at a time.

Personal Competencies

The starting point of the series is developing personal skills, given that effective self-management is essential for managing people, programs, and processes. It goes without saying that to manage others, you first must be able to manage yourself. People who are familiar with their personal strengths and challenges and who engage in effective self-management tend to work well with others.

ORGANIZING YOURSELF

Here are the competencies included in the Personal Competencies cluster:

1. **Living the Core Values**, which involves demonstrating honesty, truthfulness, trustworthiness, reliability, fairness, and ethicality in all your decisions and interactions.
2. **Developing Personal Mastery** through personal responsibility, emotional resilience, constructive attitudes, self-confidence, adaptability, conscientiousness, and competence.
3. **Organizing Yourself** by focusing on your

ORGANIZING YOURSELF

priorities and making effective use of time.
4. **Building Stress Resilience**, which deals with managing life's stresses by developing personal hardiness.

People Competencies

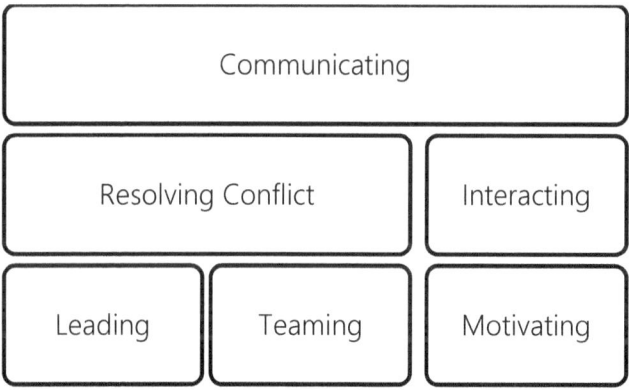

This cluster helps you examine and build your skills in working with and managing others. Although it's important for managers to be *technically* competent in order to gain credibility, interpersonal skills make the difference between awesome and not-so-awesome managers.

ORGANIZING YOURSELF

The competencies included in the People Competencies cluster are:

5. **Communicating in Writing and through Presentations**, which focuses on communicating ideas effectively, whether verbally or in writing.
6. **Creating Engagement**, creating motivating working conditions so that staff contribute their best to the organization.
7. **Building Relationships**, which considers how to interact with others through effective listening and responding.
8. **Resolving Conflict**, which addresses how to deal with conflict in a productive manner.
9. **Leading Your Team**, which means leading in a manner that is appropriate for the needs of the situation and your team.
10. **Cultivating Team Spirit** by building a cohesive, high-performing team.

ORGANIZING YOURSELF

Purpose and Process Competencies

This final cluster combines two sets of competencies. Purpose competencies offer you a "big picture" perspective of your organization and your own role in the organization. Process competencies help you translate this "big picture" (the *whats*) into everyday practice (the *hows*). In other words, they allow you to consider how work should be done as a means of accomplishing the goals of your organization and your work unit.

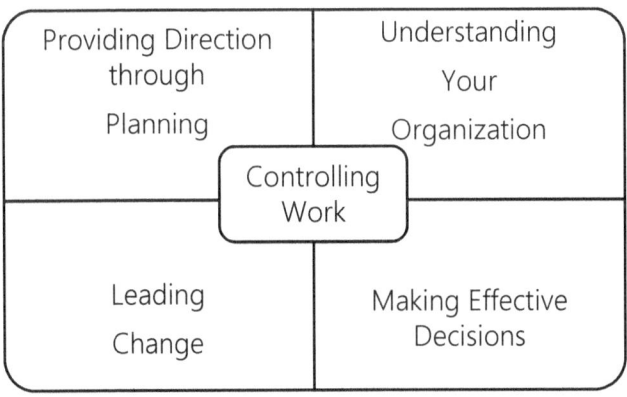

ORGANIZING YOURSELF

Purpose and Process competencies include:

11. **Making Effective Decisions**, whether individually or in a team setting.
12. **Controlling Work Performance** by establishing control mechanisms to ensure results.
13. **Providing Direction through Planning**, which discusses the management process and offers tips for setting organizational direction and developing operational plans that fit this direction.
14. **Understanding Your Organization**, in other words, understanding the principles of organizing work and creating the right structure for your work unit.
15. **Leading Change** so that your organization and team thrive.

ORGANIZING YOURSELF

How is each book organized?

Each book is organized according to a five-step learning process. This process is designed to help you learn in an active and reflective manner.

In each book, after a brief introduction, we jump right into the "**reality check**." This series of self-coaching questions is meant to help you reflect on and develop insight into your own strengths and weaknesses in relation to a particular competence and, hopefully, motivate

ORGANIZING YOURSELF

you to work on building your competencies.

The reality check consists of the kinds of questions that management coaches might ask you, but that you can simply ask yourself. Just be sure to give yourself a chance to answer them!

Management coaches help managers view and understand situations from a variety of perspectives. But, if the art of coaching is asking challenging questions (as management coach Chantal Binet says), why not ask yourself these questions?

Second, to accompany you on your learning journey, you're offered a curated collection of **inspirational quotes**. There's lots of wisdom available from people from all walks of life. The quotes that grab us and speak to us do so because they have touched a nerve in us. They resonate with us, perhaps because they offer a message that we need to hear to continue developing or because they challenge us to become better people.

ORGANIZING YOURSELF

Third, we offer you tons of **tips and tricks** of awesome managers. These practical tips cover a gamut of perspectives and actions that you can take to improve your competencies. Ideally, they will encourage you to consider the variety of possibilities and alternatives that are available to you. It's up to you to decide which are the most useful to you. As you read this section, be sure to note or highlight the tips that stand out for you.

Next, we present a series of **dilemmas** or situations for you to resolve. This section will help you see how you might apply the tips and tricks from the previous section. We ask you to read the situation and then identify what you would do in these situations. You might choose one of the alternatives that is offered, or you might come up with your own creative solution. Ultimately, there are many factors and perspectives that might influence what is the "best" choice.

ORGANIZING YOURSELF

Finally, we nudge you to develop an **action plan** that you will *actually* implement. Developing and implementing an action plan is an especially important step because it helps you draw value from your efforts in working through this series. After all, you're reading this book because you're hoping to become an awesome manager, right? This means developing a realistic plan that describes the actions that you intend to take to become an awesome manager, implementing your plan, reflecting on how well it worked, and then continuously making any adjustments that are needed. So, the cycle starts again!

ORGANIZING YOURSELF

How can you get the most out of the series?

You can read one or two books per month for an entire year, creating and implementing action plans for each book. Ultimately, this will help you develop a better understanding of yourself as a manager, your expectations, your strengths, and your areas for improvement.

As a way of refreshing your competencies, you can even re-read the books and re-visit your action plans in the future. Depending on what's happening in your life (new job, new team, new challenges), every time you read these books, you may develop new insights that help you deal with a situation.

ORGANIZING YOURSELF

The knowledge of the world is only to be acquired in the world, and not in a closet.
Lord Chesterfield

What we have to learn to do,
we learn by doing.
Aristotle

Life is a succession of lessons which must be lived to be understood.
Ralph Waldo Emerson

What do this British statesman from the 1600s, Greek philosopher from 384 B.C., and American poet from the 1800s have in common? They all agree that learning comes from trying new things, not from simply sitting back and reading a book.

Don't just read the books; *do* them! Just reading the books won't transform you into an awesome manager. If you just read the books, you might get to know a lot about what it means to be an awesome manager without changing

ORGANIZING YOURSELF

what you do in the workplace. How useful is that? Just like learning to ride a bike, it's impossible to develop your skills by simply reading or even thinking about what you have read. Besides, as *The Matrix* reminds us, "There's a difference between knowing the path and walking it."

In order to truly learn from our experiences, we need to do a complete loop of the learning cycle: we need to reflect on our experiences, figure out what lessons we learned, consider ways to apply these lessons, and then apply them. You may know people who seem to repeat the same mistakes over and over again or people who continually approach situations in a manner that doesn't work for them. It's probably because they go through life without taking the time to reflect, consider what they've learned, and develop an action plan in order to change their experiences. They're stuck somewhere on the learning cycle. David Kolb, the creator of this learning cycle, says that we all have a favorite place on the cycle where we tend

ORGANIZING YOURSELF

to get stuck.

Some people simply enjoy reading the books and reflecting on how they may relate to their lives, hopefully finding an opportunity to make use of their learning at some point in the future. However, without specific goals and action plans, they're not extracting as much value as they could from their investment of time and money.

Although this is partly due to differences in learning styles, it's also due to a reluctance to try something new and different. This may be caused by a fear of stepping out of one's comfort zone: what is familiar is comfortable. It may also be caused by a desire to accumulate a truckload of knowledge or have the perfect circumstances, such as the ideal boss or set of employees, before acting. Some of us think and think and continue to think without taking action. That used to be my personal downfall until I realized that knowing lots about a topic isn't the same as learning or making a difference in real life!

ORGANIZING YOURSELF

At the other extreme, some of us take action without first reflecting on our experiences and what we learned from them. Some people prefer to go ahead and try things out right away. They're more action-oriented than their reflective counterparts. These folks typically find it especially challenging to slow down, consciously reflect on what they're reading, and develop a well thought out action plan before acting. In the same way, if you just read the books and do nothing else, the learning process will get stuck right off the bat.

Reflecting and taking action is the best solution. It's not enough to *know* how to do something. Although it's helpful and important to take the time to reflect and develop insights, at some point, you need to *do* the work yourself. Otherwise, as management expert Peter Block has said, "Waiting becomes an excuse for not acting."

Here are **five other important things** to do to maximize your learning. First, **keep a learning journal**. Record your thoughts as you

ORGANIZING YOURSELF

read the books, answer the self-coaching questions, and develop your action plans. It will help you clarify your thinking, see patterns in what you have been experiencing and writing, and serve as a record of commitments you have made to yourself through your action plans. You'll be able to look back at what you've written and be impressed with all that you've learned! You could use a notebook or create an electronic document. Some people even email journal entries to themselves as a way of recording the day and time of their entries.

Second, **pull together a feedback team** who can help you get the most from this series. Your feedback team could be a group of four or five people that you have confidence in, such as coworkers, your manager, friends, and family members. Don't be shy about asking people for their support in helping you become a better manager; they are more willing to help you than you might think! These discussions will offer you different perspectives and exponentially increase how much you learn from the series.

ORGANIZING YOURSELF

Besides, awesome managers surround themselves with people they trust who are willing to give them honest feedback that will help them grow as individuals.

In supporting you, others can play one or more of the following roles:

→ The Head: These people can help you analyze a question or problem objectively. They can sketch out options, compare data, or simply provide you with accurate information.
→ The Heart: These people can help you express your emotions and understand them better. They listen, cheer you up, don't make judgments, and give you a sense of security.
→ The Legs/Arms: These people help you do things. They go places with you; they make you get moving when you don't feel like it. These people energize you.

How can your manager help? Can your manager provide feedback, advice and tips, and

ORGANIZING YOURSELF

time to complete the series? What will you do to get your manager's help? For example, could you meet with your manager once every two weeks to discuss your progress and talk about how to manage effectively?

How can your peers help? Can your peers provide feedback, tips about managing, or coaching when needed? What will you do to get their help? Could you schedule a coffee break with them once every two weeks to discuss what you're learning and to share tips? Can you work through the series together?

How can your employees help? Can your employees provide feedback regarding your strengths and opportunities for improvement or work with you to develop a plan for making your unit function more effectively? What will you do to get their help? Could you meet with them once every two weeks to discuss what you're learning and how your team can implement elements of your action plan?

How can your friends help? Could they provide feedback, tips about managing, and

ORGANIZING YOURSELF

encouragement for you to try new things? What will you do to get their help? Could you organize a dinner with them once every two weeks to discuss what you're learning and how to implement your action plan?

Third, **develop and implement a SMARTER action plan.** You know you've really learned something when your behavior changes (for the better, of course). Insights and tips that are meaningful to you will change your perspective *and* your behaviors. That's why each book ends by inviting you to develop an action plan. Your plan should be **Specific, Measurable, Attainable, Realistic, Timely, Exciting, and Rewarded.** Think about things that you need to start doing, stop doing, or continue doing. Here's an example: "By the end of next week, I will write two letters – one to my former manager and one to my best friend – expressing

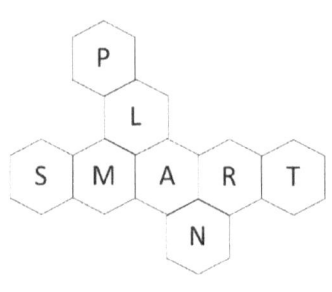

ORGANIZING YOURSELF

my gratitude for their coaching and willingness to challenge me to become a better person. I will send these letters by email no later than Friday afternoon." Write your action plan in your journal. Revisit it to check your progress, and revise your plan as needed. Remember to ask for help from others, evaluate your progress, and reward yourself for your progress toward becoming an awesome manager.

Fourth, **identify obstacles or barriers that might get in your way of making the most of the series** and implementing your action plans; for example, lack of time or energy, poor personal habits, others' expectations, etc. List these in the column labelled "Obstacles" on the following page. Now, think about specific actions that you can take to address them and place these in the "Neutralizers" column; for example, meet with your manager, plan small wins or ways to celebrate your progress, etc.

ORGANIZING YOURSELF

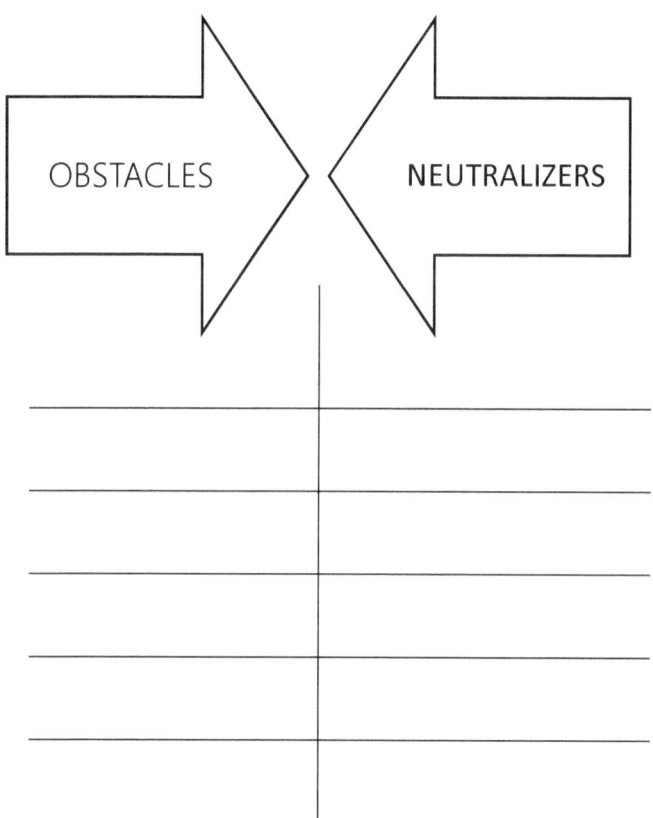

ORGANIZING YOURSELF

Finally, do what you need to do to motivate yourself. Don't wait to be motivated to get started. Instead, get started, and motivation will come knocking at your door!

Also, try to be comfortable with discomfort. As you change how you manage, you may meet with some resistance from those around you. You exist in a system of relationships. Because systems are geared toward equilibrium (stability), if you change one thing in the system, the equilibrium is shot, and the system is upset. There may be pressure from others and from your own sense of comfort for you to do what you've always done regardless of whether or not it works.

It may be tempting to give up when things feel unnatural, but rest assured that this is part of the learning process. It's normal that trying out new ways of doing things makes you feel a bit uncomfortable in one way or another. Sometimes, we come across awesome folks who do their work without hesitation and seemingly without effort. It's easy to forget that they've

ORGANIZING YOURSELF

gone through the highs and lows of the learning process. For example, think of Cirque du Soleil acrobats who seem to perform stunts with ease and pinpoint accuracy. It took them lots of practice, repetition, and even occasional failures to get to that skill level. Experts make things look easy.

Are you ready to begin your awesome journey? Earl Nightingale once said, "All you need is the plan, the road map, and the courage to press on to your destination." I hope that this series serves as your guide and road map on your journey toward awesomeness.

REFERENCES

Aid Association for Lutherans (1982). *The Stress Examiner.*

Bittel, L.R. (1991). *Right On Time: The Complete Guide for Time-Pressured Managers.* New York: McGraw-Hill.

Covey, S. (1989). *The Seven Habits of Highly Effective People.* New York: Simon & Schuster.

Lakein, A. (1989). *How to Get Control of Your Time and Your Life.* Signet.

Silberman, M. L. (1993). *Twenty Active Training Programs Volume 2.* Pfeiffer.

ORGANIZING YOURSELF

Playbooks in the Managerial Competencies Series

1. Living the Core Values
2. Developing Personal Mastery
3. Organizing Yourself
4. Building Stress Resilience
5. Communicating in Writing and through Presentations
6. Creating Engagement
7. Building Relationships
8. Resolving Conflict
9. Leading Your Team
10. Cultivating Team Spirit
11. Making Effective Decisions
12. Controlling Work Performance
13. Providing Direction through Planning
14. Understanding Your Organization
15. Leading Change

www.ingramcontent.com/pod-product-compliance
Lightning Source LLC
Chambersburg PA
CBHW070304230526
45470CB00002B/723